ZIONSVILLE INDIANA PUBLIC LIBRARY

S0-AFD-964

Chickens

Chickens

Hussey-Mayfield Memorial
Public Library
Zionsville, IN 46077

Mary Ann McDonald

THE CHILD'S WORLD®, INC.

Copyright © 1998 by The Child's World®, Inc.
All rights reserved. No part of this book may be
reproduced or utilized in any form or by any means
without written permission from the publisher.
Printed in the United States of America.

Library of Congress Cataloging-in-Publication Data
McDonald, Mary Ann.
Chickens/written by Mary Ann McDonald.
p.   cm.
Includes index.
Summary: Introduces the physical characteristics, behavior and life cycle of chickens.
ISBN 1-56766-374-5 (smythe-sewn, lib. reinforced)
1. Chickens—Juvenile literature. [1. Chickens.] I. Title.
SF487.5.M38 1997
636.5—dc21   96-46192
                              CIP
                              AC

Photo Credits

COMSTOCK/Thomas Wear: cover
COMSTOCK/Russ Kinne: 24
Robert & Linda Mitchell: 2
Joe McDonald: 9, 16, 30
Joe Cornish/Tony Stone Images: 6
Peter Dean/Tony Stone Images: 10
Bob Thomason/Tony Stone Worldwide: 13
Cathlyn Melloan: 15
William Muñoz: 19, 23, 29
ANIMALS ANIMALS: Barbara J. Wright: 20
Rob Boudreau/Tony Stone Images: 26

On the cover...

Front cover: This *white Leghorn rooster* is watching over the barnyard.
Page 2: This *red Indonesian jungle fowl* and her chicks are sitting in the grass.

Table of Contents

Cluck—Cluck! Peep–Peep! Cock-a-doodle-doo! Have you ever visited a farm and wondered what animal was making this noise? Perhaps you have held an egg from the supermarket and wondered what creature it came from. What could it be? A chicken!

Chickens are the most common kind of tame birds. Farmers like chickens because they are very easy to take care of. They don't need much space to live. Many farmers also like to raise chickens because they do not cost much money to buy. Chickens are found in every state and in almost every country of the world.

These chickens are eating on a farm in France.

What Do Chickens Look Like?

All chickens have two legs, a beak, a tail, feathers and wings. Chickens also have red fleshy growths on the top of their heads called **combes**. The red skin that hangs down under their beak is called the **wattle**. On some chickens, the comb and wattle can be very big and beautiful.

There are many different colors and shapes of chickens. Male chickens, called **roosters**, are very colorful with long beautiful feathers. Roosters also have a special claw, called a **spur**, on the back of each leg. The spur is very sharp. It is used to fight other male birds.

This rooster has many colorful feathers.

Many farmers let their chickens roam freely during the day. Chickens only need a dry, warm place to sleep at night. Chickens will sleep almost anywhere—in a shed, on hay bales, and even on the seats of tractors! Most of the time, a farm will have a special chicken barn called a **coop** to keep the chickens safe. A coop can house many chickens.

These chickens are gathering outside their coop.

Where Do Eggs Come From?

A female chicken is called a **hen**. Hens lay eggs in a nest. Some eggs develop into baby chickens called **chicks**. Most of the eggs that hens lay are unfertilized. These eggs never turn into chicks. These are the eggs that you get from the supermarket.

This unfertilized egg is just like the ones you can buy in the store.

On most farms, a special coop is made for egg-laying hens. Here the farmer will provide lots of clean, fresh straw for the hens to make their nests from. Once or twice a day the farmer collects all the unfertilized eggs from the chicken coop. The farmer then takes the eggs to the store and sells them to hungry customers.

These chickens have their nests inside the round holes under the window.

Eggs come in different colors. We buy mostly white eggs in the grocery stores. But some chicken breeds lay eggs with brown shells. And the *Araucana chicken* from Chile lays greenish blue eggs! All eggs taste the same no matter what color the shell is.

Araucana chickens like this one lay blue eggs.

What Are Chickens' Feathers Like?

Once a year, a chicken will shed its feathers—but not all at the same time. This is called **molting**. When a chicken is molting, the old feathers fall off and fresh, new feathers grow back in their place. Chickens can't fly during the molt, and hens don't lay eggs. It takes between six and ten weeks for a chicken to grow its new feathers.

While this chicken is molting, some of its feathers are long, and some are short.

How Do Chickens Clean Themselves?

Chickens love to take dust baths. They often lie on their sides and thrash around in the dirt. This helps them to clean themselves. The dirt also kills mites and lice, which are called **parasites**. Parasites make the chicken itch. Parasites can also cause some diseases which would hurt the chicken. So instead of getting the chicken dirty, dust baths are good for the chicken.

This chicken is taking a dust bath.

What Do Chickens Eat?

Chickens eat mostly grain and seed. Chickens also love to eat **mash**. Mash is a special mix of ground grains and vitamins. Different kinds of mash are fed to either egg-laying hens or to chickens that will be used for meat.

Chickens also like to eat **scratch**. Scratch is cracked or ground grain such as corn, oats or wheat. Many chickens eat grasses such as alfalfa or clover when they can't find any mash or scratch.

These hungry farm chickens are eating scratch,

Chickens can eat a lot of food. And sometimes chickens eat when they are not hungry. They can eat so much that chickens need a special pouch in their neck to store extra food. This pouch is called a crop.

Chickens don't have teeth—so how do they chew their food? Before they eat, chickens swallow tiny stones that they find on the ground. These stones sit in a special stomach called a **gizzard**. When a chicken eats, the food passes into the gizzard first before it goes to the main stomach. The stones in the gizzard grind up the food into tiny mashed pieces. Then the food is ready to travel on to the main stomach.

This *silver-spangled Hamburg fowl* is looking for small stones.

What Are Baby Chickens Like?

When a hen lays her eggs, she can tell which eggs will become chicks and which ones won't. A hen also knows that she needs to keep the fertilized eggs warm for three weeks before her chicks are born. To do this, she sits on them all day long. And to make sure that all of her eggs stay warm, the hen turns each egg once a day. While she is sitting on her eggs, a hen won't eat much. She will only leave her eggs once or twice a day.

This hen is sitting on her nest that she made in the dirt.

27

When chicks hatch they are ready to eat on their own. They learn what and how to eat by watching their mother. Hens and chicks talk to each other by using many sounds. Chicks call for their mothers with loud peeps. A hen clucks softly to say "Follow me." Loud, excited clucks means "I've found food!" And sometimes a hen will call in a high scream to her chicks. This means "Danger!"

This hen is teaching her chicks how to find food.

Chickens are very important. The eggs and meat that we get from chickens helps us grow strong and stay healthy. Chickens are also a fun farm animal to raise. So the next time you see a chicken, feed it some cracked corn. You will be it's friend for life!

This rooster is keeping watch over some other chickens.

Glossary

chick (CHIK)
A young chicken is called a chick.

comb (KOHM)
The red flesh that grows on the top of a chicken's head is called a comb.

coop (KOOP)
A coop is a special barn where chickens are housed.

gizzard (GIH–zurd)
A gizzard is a special stomach where chickens grind up their food.

hen (HEN)
A female chicken is called a hen.

mash (MASH)
Mash is a special mix of ground grains and vitamins. Barnyard chickens like to eat mash.

molting (MOHL–ting)
Birds shed their feathers once a year. This is called molting.

parasite (PARE-uh-site)
A parasite is an animal that lives and feeds on other animals. Chickens take dust baths to get rid of parasites.

rooster (ROOS–ter)
A male chicken is called a rooster.

scratch (SKRATCH)
Scratch is cracked or ground grain such as corn, oats or wheat. Chickens like to eat scratch.

spur (SPURR)
A spur is special claw on the back of a rooster's leg. Roosters use their spurs when they fight other roosters.

wattle (WA–tuhl)
The wattle is the red flesh that hangs down under a chicken's beak.

Index